How to Create Your Own
Landscape Economy

How to Create Your Own Landscape Economy

The Landscape Professionals Guide to Raising Prices & Doubling Your Income

Strategic **Landscaper**

www.StrategicLandscaper.com

Strategic Landscaper

www.StrategicLandscaper.com

Copyright © 2017 by Matt Hudson

First print edition published in 2017

ISBN-10: 1-5440-5449-1
ISBN-13: 978-1-5440-5449-0

Dedication

Melissa,

Everything in this book has your unwavering love wrapped around it. Your faith in me and support of my entrepreneurial spirit, as I faced uncertainty and heartache, has been my rock.

When I did not believe in myself, you always have. You are the most supportive and loving person on this planet.

Thank you.

I love you always.

Matt

How to Create Your Own Landscape Economy

Table of Contents

Table of Contents

Table of Contents

The Missing Pieces

Preface

The day I decided to launch my first landscape company, Eco-Scapes, in September of 1996 I thought I was embarking on an automatic path to success, freedom and prosperity. I was going to be able to work for myself, work outside every day, work with nature and make a lot of money quickly. My vision was so exciting, I was full of energy, focus and determination.

I did not have a clue what I was doing.

I believed the degree in Landscape Architecture that I was working on was the launch point for my guaranteed success. My strategy was to build up a lawn maintenance route while working towards my degree. Graduate. Start offering design-build services. Make a lot of money.

It all made perfect sense.

How could I possibly fail?

Well for starters, I did build up a profitable lawn maintenance route that pushed me through graduation and obtaining my degree. I was on to Phase Two of my plan launch my design-build services.

Unfortunately, as soon as I abandoned my lawn maintenance route "because now I had a degree in Landscape Architecture I must focus on design-build," the South experienced a severe drought and absolutely nobody was installing new landscapes.

I was broke and busted, both financially and emotionally. This was the first of many lessons and challenges that I have self-inflicted, or endured, throughout my two decades of service in the Green Industry.

The takeaway is that no matter how great your plan is, if there are holes in it they will eventually affect your business and ultimately your life.

The Only Fertilizer for Your Landscape Business

Fast forward twenty years and now I know there is only one fertilizer for a landscape business. There is only one additive that can keep your business strong, healthy and beautiful always. That is your ability to effectively market and sell your services.

This is the ultimate fertilizer for your business. When you learn how to manufacture it and apply it, you are in control of your destiny. Your path to success is always a healthy, green lawn pulling you along.

"But what about production, employee management, fleet management, taxes, scheduling, equipment mainte-nance........"

None of that matters if you don't have the **RIGHT** projects in your pipeline.

There are many important lessons and skills that you must learn and apply to successfully *create your own landscape economy*, but one of the most important that you will learn in this book is that you are no longer in the landscaping business. You are in the marketing business.

If you accept this, your future is bright with endless possibilities. If you discredit this as hype and say: "I don't need to market my business; I rely on referrals only," your future is guaranteed one thing: inconsistency.

Your ability to identify the right customers, deliver the right message to them at the right time and generate an immediate direct response (successful marketing) will guarantee the future stability of your business.

Why?

Because as some wise person once said: "The only constant is change."

And if you were in business from 2008-2010, you know how devastating sudden change can be if you are not prepared. But despite what the obnoxious and overhyped media might have told you, the world did not come to an end in 2008. There were many successful businesses that charged right through the Great Recession and captured more market share.

How?

Because they created their own economy. They knew how to market and sell their services. They adjusted their strategy to the current conditions and thrived.

The purpose of this book is to show you how to create your own economy. An economy that will allow you to reach your next goal and many more you have yet to set. If your company is already successful and you are looking for that extra edge to take your business to the next level, this book can help. If your company is flat year after year or if you are tired, lost and frustrated, not knowing what to do to create different results, this book can help.

For many, the difference between success and failure is not effort, it's the application of the right knowledge and mindset. Hard work alone will get you nowhere if you are not taking the right action with a focused, positive and confident mindset.

If you work 100 hours per week on production only, your business will most likely fail or kill you. Period.

You must become an expert at marketing and sales. When you do this, you will begin the process of creating your own economy, and your life will never be the same.

I have spent over 20 years learning and testing as a Landscape Entrepreneur. I know what it is like to be waiting on one deposit check, or a final payment, so I can put gas in my truck and feed my family. I know with all my being that if you apply the lessons in this book you will never have to experience those frustrations again.

I sincerely wish you abundant success for many years to come. There is no better time than right now to change your life forever.

 CHAPTER 1

Introduction. Who Is Matt Hudson and How Can He Help Me?

Before we dig deep into how you can *create your own landscape economy*, and change your life forever, I want to take a few moments to introduce myself and hopefully build a little trust with you. Since I was a young child, I have had a drive to be a successful entrepreneur. I did not always know what the word meant, but there has always been a drive deep down inside of me that wanted to work for myself and build an amazing business that would take care of my family and influence the world.

My parents were not entrepreneurs and I never formally studied business, but like many before me, I just hung my shingle and opened a business. My first business was a landscape company I called Eco-Scapes. I launched Eco-Scapes in the fall of 1996 in Athens, Georgia while entering my first of three years studying Landscape Architecture at the University of Georgia.

My business model consisted of taking my student loan check for the semester and buying a $3,000 Toro Deck mower, and with the little money I had left, printing off a few thousand 8.5" x 11" neon flyers and driving neighborhood to neighborhood, putting them on mailboxes. If I remember correctly I believe that ad headline used adjectives like "affordable", "quality" and "best." Not exactly professional copywriting (as if I even knew what professional copywriting was). I think I even quoted flat rates for services for all properties. What an amazing estimating system I had!

I did not have a clue about marketing, sales or building a business. But I did have a goal and determination that proved to be worth a lot.

During that semester, I successfully captured enough clients and earned enough profit to pay the bills and expenses my student loan check was intended to cover. I built up a nice maintenance route and a few simple landscaping jobs over the next three years.

The Long Road to Success

By no means was I an overnight success. After earning my degree in Landscape Architecture in the winter of 1998 I ignored the advice of my professor to get a job with and established landscape company to learn how to run a business for a few years and then launch my own company. Instead, I continued with Eco-Scapes and built a nice little business for myself. But at the end of the day I was spending most of my time on production and was slowly burning myself out. I did not understand the importance of working *on my business*, as opposed to *in my business.*

As I mentioned earlier, in 1999 I let go of my maintenance accounts and focused full time on design-build. That summer the South experienced a drought and nobody was installing new landscapes. My business model was crushed and Eco-Scapes was on life support.

But I remained persistent and over the next 9 years, I continued to run my own businesses. I designed and built landscapes, learned how to build ponds and waterfalls, learned how to design and install low-voltage lighting systems and eventually purchased a same day on-site landscape design franchise in the winter of 2008.

During this entire journey as an entrepreneur the one thing that I was most consistent about was my thirst for knowledge. I knew that I did not know what I did not know, and rather than that keeping me from acting, it motivated me to read more books, listen to more Nightingale-Conant audio programs and continue to learn about business and personal development.

I had, and still have, an unquenchable thirst for knowledge, personal development and business strategy. I am constantly driven to reach the next goal, to learn more and build a better life for myself and my family.

The culmination of these past 20 years has led me to this book and sharing a business system for landscape professionals that can transform your life and allow you to reach your business goals month after month and year after year. I have tried and failed. I have succeeded and then failed. But I have never given up, and now I am practicing this very strategy and producing amazing and lasting results for my businesses.

During my 20+ year career, I have taken one small landscaping company and doubled its sales in the first 12 months from $600k to $1.2M, and taken another company from a

.001% net profit margin to a 15% net profit margin within 12 months.

From everything I have experienced, lasting success does not come without effort. Of course, there may be an exception to any rule or circumstance, but what I am talking about is creating a business that provides the resources, gratification and profits that change your life forever. This level of success must be earned; it must start in your mind and be fulfilled with your actions.

The purpose of this book is to provide you with a blueprint to *create your own landscape economy: how to raise your prices and double your income.* These are bold statements I know, but that is the point. This book is about helping you shift your view of business to one where you create your business environment on your terms and fully enjoy the rewards of your efforts.

It can be done. It is being done every day by amazing business owners around the world. At the end of the day it comes down to knowledge, mindset, belief and action. My goal is for you to be able to apply this blueprint, and *create your own landscape economy.*

How to Use This Book

Please take the time to read this book once to get an understanding of the concepts. Then I recommend you read it at least two more times. Take notes. Study.

This book is filled with concepts, strategies and tactics that you may not be familiar with. To *create your own landscape economy*, you must invest time, money and energy over an extended period to reap the rewards. The value you seek cannot be obtained with shortcuts or quick fixes. You are building an economy. You are doing something that 99% of all business owners do not even know about. You will be creating something very special and it requires effort and focus.

With that said, I have no doubt that you can do this. You can be abundantly successful. You can create your own economy. You can transform your life to one of abundance, power, control and passion. You can (and should) have a blast doing it.

No matter what the television tells you, you live in an amazing time of abundance and opportunity. There are more millionaires and billionaires in this world today than ever before in human history. It doesn't matter where you came from; all that matters is where you are going.

Now is the time. Trust yourself and believe in yourself because if you don't, no one else will.

Now let's learn how to *create your own landscape economy*.

How to Create Your Own Landscape Economy

 CHAPTER 2

Create Your Own Landscape Economy

Your interest in *creating your own landscape economy* says that you are looking for a way to improve your business, your career and your quality of life. You would not be reading this right now otherwise. It also says that you are looking to create a landscape business that you control as opposed to so many landscape businesses that control their owners and slowly grind them down. Well I have good news for you. It is happening every day, and you too can *create your own landscape economy* much faster and easier than you may currently believe.

Creating your own landscape economy is about freedom, peace of mind, independence and prosperity. It's about waking up every day excited for the day's work ahead because you are in control of your business, and no matter what the day throws at you, you know that your business is built to last. It's about having an internal belief in yourself, a knowing that you are responsible your success. It's about knowing that no matter how bad the economy gets or how stiff the competition becomes you have the ability, knowledge and resources to thrive, yes thrive.

What I am describing to you is not hype. It is not imagined concepts that are great to think about but impossible to achieve. What I am describing to you is possible and you can achieve it when you gather the correct information and put it into action with unshakeable belief in yourself.

Which is exactly the purpose of this book—to help you transform your business so that you are no longer subject to the grind and frustrations that are so common in our industry. There is a way to design and build your business so that you can create a lifestyle that is in direct alignment with your priorities, goals and vision.

Reality Check

WARNING: If you are sensitive to harsh and honest observations you might find this section offensive.

I've laid out what's possible, now let's have an honest discussion about what it will take to get there. The reason so few landscape entrepreneurs *create their own landscape economy* is because they either don't know how (which is most likely the case) or they don't have the patience, focus and discipline to bring the information to life. Creating a business that is insulated from circumstances, a business where you can choose whom you want to work with and at what price does not happen automatically. It requires a lot of work, attention to detail, implementation and belief in yourself. For these reasons, most landscape entrepreneurs will never *create their own landscape economy* it's just not going to happen. Most landscape entrepreneurs will grind away, chasing checks, experiencing the peaks and valleys of seasonal cash flow and exposed to the tides of the larger economies.

The question comes down to whether you are willing to invest the time, money, energy and resources to *create your own economy*. Are you willing to push yourself to places you have never been? Are you willing to take long, hard looks at yourself and be honest about your strengths and weaknesses? Are you willing to accept the feedback that is your life and change the "you" who created it?

I have some very harsh but real information for you to process. If you are unhappy with parts, or all, of your business and/or life you only have yourself to blame. You created it. Not the economy. Not your partner. Not your low bid competitors. YOU. And the only way you will have the life of your dreams is to change you and your actions.

So, what are you going to do about it? Are you going to keep taking the same actions that have brought you to where you are and expect your results to be different? Or are you going to open your mind, seek new information, put a plan together, get focused and *create your own landscape economy*?

I make no apologies for these statements because they are as true for me as they are for you. It was this awareness and realization of ultimate responsibility and accountability that allowed me to shift my mindset and change my actions resulting in better results for me, my businesses and my life. My job with this book is to help you achieve something so extraordinary that 99% of your competitors and industry peers will never accomplish and if I simply present another business strategy with great potential without mentioning the underlying causes, I would not be serving you.

I invite you to take a hard look at your life, decide what you like and create more of that. Decide what you want to change and be willing to make whatever sacrifice necessary to get the results you desire.

It's a Simple Choice

I am here to tell you that it is 100% possible to build a company that works for you. I repeat, to build a company that works for you—a company that serves your needs and wants. A company that makes your dreams come alive. A company that is enjoyable to work at each and every day. A company that makes you smile and feel secure.

Now I have no idea how you feel about your business. I don't know if you are young, energetic and enthusiastic about the future or a 30-year landscape veteran looking for a comfortable way to retire. Regardless of where you fall on this spectrum, you can benefit from the system taught in this book. The lifestyle of *creating your own landscape economy can happen* for you, and it can happen sooner rather than later. It's simply a matter of committing to the process and trusting yourself to reach your goal.

You can do this.

CHAPTER 3

Build Your Marketing & Sales Machine

To *create your own landscape economy,* the starting point is to continually attract and keep great customers. To first *attract* great customers, you must have an automated marketing and sales system that consistently generates great customers. To *keep* great customers, you must have an automated marketing and sales system that consistently and effectively communicates with your existing customers and keeps them for the life of your business.

Now let me be clear, when I say "automated" I don't mean a system that requires absolutely no work—that would be ridiculous. The automation I am talking about is a SYSTEM that is designed, built and managed to consistently create highly targeted leads (marketing) that convert into great customers (sales). A system that you can count on week after week, month after month and year after year: a marketing and sales machine.

The marketing and sales machine you are going to learn in this book will work for any Green Industry business. Yes, any Green Industry business. It doesn't matter if your business is B2B or B2C, it works for both. If you think your business is different, you are wrong. Your business is not unique. Your business does not defy the natural laws of business. To *create your own landscape economy* the first step is to create your marketing and sales machine.

With that said, there is one requirement for your marketing and sales machine to work. You must take massive action. You must be willing to put in the time and effort to build, adjust, monitor, maintain and fine tune your marketing and sales machine. This process never ends. It's like eating. If you stop eating, you die. If you stop feeding your marketing and sales machine at some point, your business will start to die, either from natural causes, poor health or environmental impact.

How to Launch Your Landscape Marketing & Sales Machine

The following is a very simple process to launching your marketing and sales machine. Warning: The following process is simple but not always easy.

Step One: Study

Study this book and other marketing and sales resources at StrategicLandscaper.com, to learn this marketing & sales system for your landscape business. Take the time to read this book at least twice. If you are a note taker, take notes. Give this study process the attention, focus and importance it requires.

Step Two: Take Massive Action

This next step is the point in time where you will begin to leave your competition in the dust. This is the place where you separate your landscape business from 90% of others. The reason there are so few extraordinary landscape businesses is because most are stuck in production mode and chasing checks. They fail to take massive action to build the systems necessary to become truly amazing, independent and in control. Step Two is to take massive action and begin the process of creating your marketing and sales machine.

Step Three: Analyze Results

Metrics put your landscape business on steroids. The next step is to *know your numbers*. Track and analyze your results. This is where many landscape businesses come up short. They don't know their numbers. They throw time, energy and money at their business but they cannot quantify their results. It is critical that you finish the process by tracking and analyzing every marketing and sales dollar you spend to know your Return on Investment (ROI). These numbers will allow you to scale your business quickly.

Step Four: Take Informed Action

You have probably heard the saying that defines insanity as doing something over and over and expecting different results.

Fortunately for you, that is what your competition is doing. Whether it's ego, ignorance or a strong combination of both, many landscape professionals make the same mistakes repeatedly and wonder why their business is flat, why they continue to struggle and why their life never changes. Applying the lessons learned from your metrics and taking informed action allows you to learn from your past investments and create a better, faster, more responsive, and prosperous landscape business.

Step Five: Repeat Steps 3 & 4 Forever

Simple, but not always easy.

Let's Talk Marketing

Ask 10 people what role marketing plays in their business and how they feel about marketing and you will most likely hear 10 different beliefs about marketing. Here are three perspectives that I have observed from landscape professionals over the years. Unfortunately, the first two are most common:

1. Marketing is a waste of time and money. All I need is "word of mouth" to grow my business. —Wrong.

2. Marketing is necessary but I don't have time to keep up with it. —Huge mistake.

3. Marketing is the primary source for my company's growth and I have a clear process and plan for marketing my business. A plan that consistently produces a positive ROI that I can track and quantify every time. I love marketing because with marketing, I can *create my own economy*. —Correct.

Regardless of what you think about gravity, it will always bring you back to earth when you jump. Regardless of what you think about marketing, it is directly responsible for the growth, or lack of growth, of your business. Your feelings and beliefs about the necessity of marketing are irrelevant. You need marketing to grow your business and *create your own landscape economy*. What marketing looks like and what marketing system you implement is open for discussion, but the fact that you need marketing to grow your business is a fact.

Consider another fact for a moment. You are always marketing your business whether you spend a nickel on advertisements or not. You are marketing your business by the way you answer your phone. You are marketing your business by how responsive you are to your customers. You are marketing your business by the amount of detail you put into your services. You don't have to spend a lot of money to market your business. In fact, if you do not have any money to spend on advertising there are still infinite ways you can market your business.

Many successful landscape businesses have spent very little on advertising over the years. But that does not mean they have not invested in marketing their business.

How much you successfully invest into marketing—either time, money or both—will directly affect the speed at which you can scale your business and *create your own landscape economy.*

Successful marketing is a mindset and a commitment to the 5-step process outlined above. It's not complicated. It's simple, just not always easy (Have I said that yet?).

Marketing Saves Lives

Yes, marketing (done correctly) really does save lives. I'm not being facetious. Your ability to effectively market your business and generate consistent ROI for every marketing dollar you spend will directly affect your quality of life and the lives of those around you.

Ignoring marketing will make your life harder. Simple fact. Kind of like gravity when you jump out of a plane without a parachute...

The day you clearly understand that you are no longer in the landscape business, but rather in the marketing business will be the first day of a new level of abundance and opportunity you have never known. This is true. Very true.

If you are not at least open to this statement, close this book and give it to your competitors because nothing else you learn in this book will matter.

For the information in this book to improve your quality of life, it must be successfully applied and you must understand that it is successful marketing that changes everything. Marketing is the first step in this process not the last, but if you fail to successfully and consistently market your business, you cannot *create your own landscape economy.*

This book will teach you a proven system that will attract the right prospects for your business, help you convert those targeted prospects into customers, sell existing customers more products and services more frequently, lose fewer customers to competitors, generate more referrals, engage past customers to repurchase and much more.

This book will teach you how to *create your own landscape economy* and design and implement the life you dream of. This is not hyperbole. This is fact. Money, you can literally take to the bank. I have used this strategy with abundant success. I have tried and failed with many other "systems," bells and whistles or hacks.

Remember, marketing done correctly can save your life because it can exponentially increase your income, resources and abilities to respond to challenges and unforeseen circumstances. It could be as simple as affording the best health insurance or only working 30 hours a week for 20 years as opposed to 60 hours a week for 40 years.

Marketing (done correctly) can save your life.

What Profitable Marketing Looks Like

Profitable marketing, marketing with a positive ROI (the only marketing that matters), starts with generating a targeted response (a lead), converts the lead into a customer and continues to market to that customer to ensure that customer never gets away. This strategy of marketing comes from *direct marketing* which we will review in depth in Chapter 5. Successfully implement direct marketing year after year and you will reach your business goals and never again rely on outside forces to generate your business success. You will have successfully *created your own landscape economy*.

Let's Talk Sales

A sale is the exclamation point that follows your marketing. Without it your marketing is just a bunch of words with little value. But the sale changes everything. It quantifies your marketing, and it quantifies your sales process.

Did you catch those last two words? *Sales process.*

Sales rarely happen automatically. They require focus, effort and energy just like most things of value.

I recently had a client tell me they interviewed two different landscape companies, mine and a competitor's. The competitor was a well-known author on local plants and highly recommended. But when they called the company, the salesman they sent out was not the owner of the company, the author, but rather a salesman, which is completely understandable. The client told me that they chose my company over the local author's company because their sales rep spent the entire consultation talking about politics and himself. He was just winging it.

He did not understand sales. He did not have a process. He woke up in the morning and drove from appointment to appointment and hoped he sold a project based on his politics and personality.

What a complete waste of time.

His sales process immediately eliminated 50% of all prospects by talking politics, and many of the others by talking about himself.

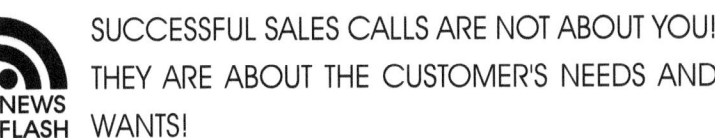 SUCCESSFUL SALES CALLS ARE NOT ABOUT YOU! THEY ARE ABOUT THE CUSTOMER'S NEEDS AND WANTS!

For your marketing and sales machine to work, for you to *create your own landscape economy,* you must have a proven sales system that will allow you to close a higher percentage of sales and grow your business. In Chapter 11, we will review how to develop a custom sales process that works for your business and your personality.

Your Custom Marketing & Sales Machine

Marketing & sales go together like peanut butter & jelly. You need both to produce the desired result, which in this case is your own landscape economy. To *create your own landscape economy,* you need a custom marketing & sales machine. Your machine will look different than my machine and that is by design. There is not a one size fits all marketing & sales system for landscape professionals that will exactly match your business's goals, and anyone who tries to tell you otherwise is mistaken. Don't take the bait.

Your custom marketing & sales machine must reflect your personality, goals and business model. The important fact is that you have a marketing & sales machine that you can use month after month, season after season, year after year to produce a predictable and profitable ROI for your business.

Now that we have established the importance of building your own custom marketing & sales machine next we are going to review a topic that directly influences the development and implementation of your marketing & sales machine, establishing a winning plan. See you in the next chapter.

How to Create Your Own Landscape Economy

 CHAPTER 4

Your Goals Need a Plan

One of my favorite sports commentators Herman Edwards once said: "A goal without a plan is a wish."

You need goals and you need a plan if you want to *create your own landscape economy*.

"I'm making money" is not a long-term sustainable strategy. Don't get me wrong, making money is a key part of creating your own economy, but when the general economy takes a dive and you are not in control of your business goals and strategy, you are subject to the effects of the economy as opposed to living in your own economy. Remember, the goal of this book is to *create your own landscape economy* so you will be in control of your business regardless of outside factors and conditions. You will have goals and the plan to reach your goals always.

Establish Your Annual Budget

At the dawn of each New Year, many landscape entrepreneurs write out their business financial goals, but many fail to officially incorporate them into a budget. Just saying, "I want to gross $1.5 million in sales with a 20% net profit margin next year" has no real value unless you can quantify how you will get there, and incorporating your goals into an annual budget is a necessary first step.

Without a budget, you are guessing as to how you will reach your financial goals. With your goals incorporated into your budget, you gain valuable insights into how you can reach your goals. A strategic plan begins to unfold and red flags from faulty assumptions will appear, which will help you determine if your goals are realistic in relation to your budget or if you need to adjust your budget to help you reach your goals.

For example, if you grossed $1M in total sales from your business the previous year and your goal is to increase gross sales to $1.5M for the upcoming year, your cost of goods, and most likely your labor, will increase. If your labor force was at peak capacity for the previous year, you will need to hire additional workers, possibly purchase additional equipment, etc. These factors will have a direct effect on profitability, which you can quantify and plan for in your budget.

By incorporating your goals into your annual budget, you can create a clear picture of what you want to achieve and how you are going to get there. Again, the goal of "I just want to make a lot of money" never works, believe me, I spent a decade chasing this "goal" and it turned out to be a wish.

Start Now

No matter what time of year you are reading this, if you do not have a 12-month annual budget in place you must stop and create one immediately. This is the foundation and road map of your plan that will drive your future successes.

If you have never created an annual budget, no worries. There are plenty of resources to help you create your first one.

Since the Green Industry is such a seasonal business, I highly recommend that you develop your annual budget month by month so you can plan for your busy seasons and your slow seasons accordingly. If you use QuickBooks there will be a wealth of metrics you can use to generate your budget month by month. If you can run an accurate profit and loss (P&L) report for the past 12 months of your business, you can use that as your guide to establishing your budget.

Again, your budget establishes your financial goals which is a key step towards *creating your own landscape economy*. If you do not have an active 12-month annual budget in place get to work and start one.

Your Marketing Budget

In your annual budget, there should be an expense line item called Advertising & Marketing, where you will set your annual budget for advertising & marketing. I recommend that your budget for advertising & marketing be 2-5% of gross sales, depending on how aggressive you want to be.

A word of caution: If you chose to spend 4-5% of your gross sales on marketing, make sure you have the sales & production systems in place to deliver a quality product and exceptional customer experience. If you successfully invest 5% of your gross sales into marketing and generate leads that you cannot deliver on, you can do as much damage as good. So be cautious if necessary. If you have a sales team ready to take calls then by all means go for it, but if you are the marketing, sales, administration and production departments then I recommend you start with 2% of your budget and generate more manageable growth.

Build Your Marketing Plan

After establishing your annual marketing budget it's time to develop your marketing plan to make it happen. With your monthly budget set, you can now determine which marketing tactics and campaigns you want to implement to help you reach (or hopefully exceed) your annual sales goals.

Again, this is a simple process, just maybe not exactly easy your first time through. But once you consistently implement your marketing plan for a year it will become second nature to you for the rest of your professional career.

Quick side note: At this point in this book I have not presented the strategy from which you will select the marketing tactics and campaigns to create your annual marketing plan. Don't get bogged down trying to figure out what marketing to implement now. The important takeaway from this chapter is understanding how to budget for your marketing plan and start from there.

When you finish this book, you should come back to this chapter and read it again and you will have the knowledge to answer the questions you may have. I have presented the information in this order because this is the order in which you will implement your marketing strategy once you understand each step.

Again, simple but not always easy. Embrace the challenge. I promise you your competition is not going to do it!

Seasonal Marketing Calendar

All Green Industry businesses have a seasonal nature to them, and it's important to leverage this fact when marketing to your customers and generating new leads. Depending on where you live, you will have different busy seasons, but regardless there will be times of the year where you are in higher demand than others.

For example, in South Florida, where our business is located, our maintenance division is most busy during the summer months because the landscapes are growing so fast and require a lot of attention. But our Design-Build Division goes almost dormant in the summer months because our population is reduced by half, the locals are traveling and it is very hot.

Knowing this, we spend a lot of time and energy marketing to commercial installation projects to fill our summer months for our Design-Build Division. At the same time during the summer months, we focus our marketing on picking up new maintenance customers because we know this is when other companies struggle to keep up and we capitalize on that.

The point is, you need to take time to look at your business through the calendar year and identify your busy and slow months for each service you offer. Once you have broken this down, you can begin building your annual marketing calendar season by season.

Season by Season, Service by Service

Now that you know your annual and monthly budget for marketing and have identified the seasonal peaks and valleys for each service you offer, the next step is to build out your seasonal marketing calendar for each service you want to promote.

The amount of money you can invest will drive the number of services you can promote and the tactics you use to promote them. Again, we will dive deep into the mechanics of seasonal campaign examples later, but for now we want to identify which services we want to promote and when.

Review the master list of services you offer. Identify one that you want to promote first. This might be landscape maintenance services because you want to build a route to maximum capacity, it might be design services in the spring and fall when they are in most demand, it could be irrigation repair services in the summer when it is very hot. Pick the first service category that you want to promote and start there.

Next, you want to go back to your calendar and determine which of the four seasons you want to market this service and why. For irrigation services, you may run a marketing campaign in the spring that talks about turning the system back on after the winter shut down. In the summer, you might promote maintenance service contracts & installation, and in the fall, you will promote maintenance services and winterizing systems.

You see, each service will have a different message for each season based on the needs of the customer. The last thing you want to do is run 20,000 postcards of the same message and send them out 12 months a year. You will probably get some work, but you will be wasting a lot of money and leaving a lot of money on the table because you are not specific and focused with your message. Just because everyone else is marketing this way doesn't mean you should waste your money copying them.

The goal with an annual marketing calendar is to identify the services you offer, look at them through the entire calendar year and break them down season by season so you can create a unique marketing message that will produce a higher ROI. As you continue to study this book, you are going to learn how to craft your messages and make sure you are reaching the right audience, but for now, I want you to understand that your annual marketing calendar should be broken down into seasons, and ultimately month by month, based on your location and the services you choose to offer. Finally, you will create seasonal marketing campaigns based on your budget and goals you want to achieve. *For more information on seasonal marketing campaigns, see Chapter 12.*

What you might discover is that the first time through may seem a little overwhelming. There will be a lot of parts to this process and your brain will be processing a lot of new information. Do not give up! Stick with it and get that first annual calendar created and then implement it.

Remember, you are now in the marketing business, not the landscaping business. For your business to consistently grow and *create your own landscape economy,* you need a steady flow of sales throughout the year, and the most effective way to plan this is with an annual marketing calendar.

See you in the next chapter where you are going to learn about direct marketing and how it will change your life forever (if you apply it).

 CHAPTER 5

Learn Direct Marketing

Okay so you have your financial goals set—you've incorporated them into your annual budget; you have a line item for advertising & marketing, which is your marketing budget; you've identified which services you want to market each season and you have a rough outline for your marketing plan/calendar. Now what?

Now you need to design, build, implement and test the marketing campaigns that will finalize your marketing plan/calendar for the upcoming year. These campaigns, when implemented correctly, will promote your services, generate leads, close sales and help you reach your financial goals. Simple, right?

Before you call up Google and give them access to your double points Visa, there are a few very important points about the do's and don'ts of marketing a landscape company that you must understand:

1. Ignore the marketing you see from your competitors and other "industry leaders." They have it all wrong.

2. Ignore the marketing you see from large corporations. They have a completely different business model and set of goals than you. You are not a large corporation.

3. Invest the time and energy necessary to become an expert direct marketer.

Your Competitors Have It All Wrong

Harsh Reality: 99% of landscape companies do not have a strategy for, or understand, what effective and profitable marketing is or even looks like. What typically happens is a business owner will decide they need to invest in some form of marketing or advertising to generate new business so they do one or both of the following:

1) They look around at their competitors and see what they are doing. Then they copy them. They figure "if it's working for them it will work for me." This includes building a website, placing an ad in a local newspaper or magazine, etc.

2) They pick a media outlet, whether it's Google, Direct Mail, Magazine, etc., and call the sales-person thinking "they must know what they are doing and they will help me build a campaign that will work."

For 99% of all Landscape Entrepreneurs this is their "strategy," they have no idea what they are doing and they are not investing the time to become a marketing expert for their business. They are relying on others to design their marketing campaigns for them. I can tell you in the best-case scenario they may get a few calls because of timing and demand, but quite often the campaigns are a flop and thus they develop a natural dislike for marketing and either conclude that "marketing doesn't work" or "all I really need is to rely on word of mouth marketing" both of which are huge mistakes and, in many cases, are the slow and inevitable death of a company.

Does any of this ring a bell for you? If so, keep reading because I have good news for you!

You Are Not a Large Corporation, so Don't Act Like One

The next most common mistake landscape entrepreneurs make is they copy the marketing & advertising strategies of large corporations. The important thing to understand about how large corporations invest in marketing & advertising is that they have completely different goals and objectives than you, the small business owner. Also, they have enormous budgets from which to invest.

Let's use Coca Cola as an example. Coca Cola is a world brand; they are known around the world by most people on the planet. Their marketing campaigns are often designed to strengthen their brand with the public, stay in front of their audience, appease their board of directors, impress Wall Street, impress the media and sell something.

Frequently you will see corporate marketing campaigns as simple as placing their logo on a highly visible billboard with no offer or details. Maybe a smiling front man with a big smile and a catchy slogan attached. Their goal with the billboard is to strengthen their brand and sell more products at some point, but they will never be able to quantify exactly how much Coca Cola they have sold from that billboard. They cannot quantify an exact ROI from that ad campaign.

You are not a large corporation so don't act like one. When you invest thousands of dollars into a direct mail campaign (which I highly recommend), don't mimic Coca Cola by just throwing your business name, pretty picture, phone number and catchy slogan that says "been in business for 25 years" and send them out. This is brand advertising and it's a huge waste of time, energy and money when applied by landscape companies. The same goes for an ad in a magazine, newspaper, your website and all other media you select to promote your landscape company.

Failure to heed this warning will cause you a lot of pain and cost you a lot of money.

Mandate: Become an Expert Direct Marketer

If you are serious about *creating your own landscape economy*, then the most important lesson you will take away from this book is that you must become an expert direct marketer. Becoming an expert direct marketer will change your business and your life because it is the only skill you can learn that can directly influence the quantity and quality of projects and clients, you can secure each and every year.

There is only one skill that can exponentially grow your business, and that is becoming an expert marketer. Nothing else. End of story. You can be the best landscaper since God himself, but if you don't know how to effectively market your business, your business trajectory will be low and your pace of growth will be slow. Low and slow is great if you are cruising the urban streets on the weekend, but it's not how you want your business to grow.

By now you may be asking, "What is direct marketing?"

The purpose of direct marketing, and what makes it more effective than other forms of marketing, is to directly connect with a consumer and directly connect the consumer to the marketer by collecting their contact information. This direct connection allows the marketer to establish an ongoing communication to drive the consumer into an organized process that presents a yes-or-no purchase decision, an appointment with a salesperson or a visit to a physical sales location. (Kennedy, 2013)

You see, direct marketing is about making an immediate connection to your target market and making strategic offers that can be tracked, monitored and quantified to determine exactly how effective the marketing campaign is working. There is no guess work with direct marketing. Results rule.

Becoming an expert direct marketer will not happen overnight but it's not impossible either. It's like every other skill you have learned in your life—you crawl, walk then run. The good news is the worst direct marketing is going to be miles ahead of any other marketing you have been implementing to this point. So, relax and take massive action to learn how to become an expert direct marketer. I promise it will pay off many times over in many ways.

Principles of Direct Marketing

We've established that direct marketing is about connecting with your target audience, capturing their contact information and making them an offer or offers to get them to either purchase now, contact a salesperson or visit a physical location. That's the general structure and goal of direct marketing but to ensure the success of every campaign I want to provide you an outline of The Direct Marketing Principles that you should incorporate in every direct marketing campaign you implement. (Kennedy, 2013)

As you continue to study this book you will learn more about these principles and how to apply them but for now, let's review The Principles of Direct Marketing:

1. *Offers*: You will make an offer or offers on all marketing and advertising materials

2. *Call to Action*: There will be a call to action with a reason to respond immediately

3. *Clear Instructions*: Provide clear instructions

4. *Metrics*: You will track, measure and analyze all results

5. *Follow Up*: Follow up, follow up, follow up

6. *Copywriting*: You will use professional copywriting

7. *Consistency*: You will implement direct marketing campaigns consistently.

When you are designing your next marketing campaign reference this list before, during and after your campaign to keep you on track and help you become an expert direct marketer.

How to Become an Expert Direct Marketer

So, I've challenged you to become an expert direct marketer and hopefully provided you with good enough examples and framework for you to want to do so. But how exactly do you become an expert direct marketer?

The first step is committing to the goal. The second step is gathering the right information. Reading books, studying, online resources and asking questions. The third step is to design, build and implement direct marketing campaigns. This is where you gain the real-world lessons. You invest your money and you analyze your returns; you tweak the system and you launch another direct marketing campaign applying what you learned.

There are no shortcuts. It is not a linear path. You are going to have other challenges and obstacles get in your way, distract you and seem more important. This is exactly why your competitors are not doing it. It's not hard; it's just not always easy. In the end, it really comes down to two things: commitment to the goal of being an expert direct marketer and management of your time.

By making this goal as important or more important than paying your bills, or day-to-day production, you will shorten your learning cycle and begin to see the lasting results you desire. I can go on for days about the importance of becoming an expert direct marketer, but it's up to you to decide if you want to *create your own landscape economy* or repeat the same results year after year.

 CHAPTER 6

A Marketing Formula You Can Count On

At this point we have discussed the concept of *creating your own landscape economy*, the importance of creating your custom marketing & sales machine, how to create an annual budget and marketing calendar, and becoming an expert direct marketer. This is the foundation for *creating your own landscape economy*, and now it is time to review actionable strategies you can implement to generate the desired results that will *create your own landscape economy* and change your business and life forever.

In this chapter, I am going to present a marketing formula you can use for your seasonal marketing campaigns. This formula, when implemented correctly, will generate targeted leads, sales and growth for your landscape business.

I learned this formula from the great marketer and influencer Dan Kennedy, and it has changed the way I market my business and exponentially improved my profits. I've modified the formula slightly based on my experiences. It works like this:

Market + Message + Media + Metrics = Profitable Marketing Campaign

Now before I dig deep into each of these components, I want you to know that when developing a direct marketing campaign with this formula, the process is not always linear. Meaning, you don't always start with identifying your market and then add your message and then add the media, etc.

In some circumstances, you might start with your metrics, which lead you to a unique message, which leads you to your target market and so forth. This is an important note as you create multiple campaigns and gain experience with this process.

With that said, when starting out I have found it useful to focus on each ingredient in a sequential order as listed above for the first few campaigns. I do this to create simplicity while my brain is adapting to this new process and way of thinking. It gives me the structure and organization I need to follow this formula through completion.

Why This Marketing Formula Works

The reason this marketing formula is so effective is simple really; it's because it connects your target market with the right message via the correct media and uses metrics to clearly define the profitability of the campaign. Let's look at each of the components of this formula and examine why each one is important and why when the formula is implemented correctly, it consistently produces effective, efficient and profitable results.

Market: A list you target to promote your products and/ or services. When you clearly identify your market, your target audience, you can craft a very focused and deliberate message that will speak to their needs and wants and select the correct media to deliver that message. Knowing and understanding your target market is crucial to the success of this formula and any marketing campaign.

Message: A precise marketing message that separates you from your competitors and speaks directly to the needs and wants of your target market. Your message will communicate who you are, your offers and why the prospect should do business with you. Your message is the component of this formula that captures the attention of your target. Your message should be engaging, exciting and provide value. The worst mistake you can make is for your message to be boring and easily overlooked.

Media: The delivery mechanism that physically connects your message to your target market. Knowing how to select the right media for your target market is a critical component to ensuring that your message is delivered correctly. A great message falling on the wrong ears is useless and a waste of time, energy and money. Don't fall victim of using the popular media of the time. This has happened frequently over the past few years with the onslaught of digital media platforms. I hope you haven't wasted too much money here.

Metrics: The analytics from your marketing campaigns that tell you what's working and what's not. This is the final component of the marketing formula which quantifies the success or failure of your campaign. Your ability to accurately collect, analyze and use the metrics from your direct marketing campaigns will have a profound effect on your ability to adjust and increase your returns on future campaigns. Ignoring the metrics is like ignoring high blood pressure—it will eventually catch up with you. Whether you are a numbers person or not, you need to find a way to embrace the metrics so you can generate the highest ROI from your marketing dollars.

Profitable Marketing Campaign: The result of generating more profits than expenses from the life of your marketing campaign. The important item to note here is that you want to consider the *lifetime value* of your marketing campaign. You may run a campaign that costs you $1,000 and only make one sale to a customer where you only earn a net profit of $800. Upon initial review, you might think this was a losing campaign and abandon ship but that might be a mistake. You need to track and analyze if you get additional future sales from this customer, or if they refer you to their neighbor who you make an additional $1,500 from. Knowing the average lifetime value of your customers can provide great insights into the profitability of your marketing campaigns.

Implementation RULES!!!

Know the marketing formula is the first step. Understanding the marketing formula is the second step. Implementing the marketing formula is the final step. To know and understand the formula without implementation is useless.

There are many reasons that landscape entrepreneurs will fail to apply this formula. For some, they will say it's a lack of time, others will claim a lack of resources, and others will simply be afraid of attracting too much work (this one I have never figured out). There will be many reasons to ignore this formula, but none of them are valid. If your goal is to grow your business, you must attract new customers and this marketing formula will do just that. It's not the only marketing formula that works, but it's the one I am recommending so you can *create your own landscape economy.*

But you must commit to the process. You must know that results will vary. You must be willing to test, adapt and test again. But the beauty of all this is that your business will grow; you will create new opportunities.

Over the next four chapters, you will learn in detail about each of the four components of this marketing formula and how to apply them. In the next chapter, we are going to discuss how to identify your Target Market.

 CHAPTER 7

Target Market. Sharpen Your Focus

Identify Your Target Market

One of the worst mistakes I see in the landscape industry, and frankly in many other industries as well, is when small business owners waste a lot of money sending out direct mail campaigns to entire zip codes. When I receive a lawn care promotional postcard in my mailbox at my town home where I don't have a lawn, I just shake my head and say a quick prayer for that business owner and hope that he survives his ignorance.

Before you spend a penny on marketing your business, it's critical that you *identify your target market* with as much detail as possible. The more targeted and fine-tuned your understanding of your Target Market, the greater your ROI is going to be.

Create Avatars of Your Best Clients

Depending on the focus of your business, you will most likely have multiple target markets based on the services you offer. Your ideal landscape maintenance customer will have different priorities and needs than your landscape design customer. Your irrigation service contract customer will have different priorities and needs than your landscape lighting customer.

The first step to identifying a target market is to identify which service you want to promote. The next step is to create an avatar of the ideal client you want to attract. An avatar is defined by Merriam-Webster's Dictionary as: *someone who represents a type of person, an idea, or a quality.*

Your avatar is a description of the characteristics of your ideal customer, and the first place you want to look to develop an avatar for your target market is at your existing customers who use the product or service you want to promote. If you want to grow your landscape maintenance route, examine a list of all your current and past landscape maintenance customers.

As you examine this list, identify your best customers, the customers with whom you enjoy working with. The customers whom you are most grateful for. The customers who pay on time, pay the best, live in an area that is most convenient for you, have properties that are profitable to maintain and any other criteria that is important to you.

Once you have a list of your best landscape maintenance customers, you want to dig deep into that list and write down everything you know about them: name, age, marital status, political views, occupation, income, gender, religious views, hobbies, vacations they take, if they have a second home, how many kids do they have, how old their children are, etc.

Once you have this information developed, study it and see where the opportunities lie. I once realized that many of my best design-build customers, who spent the most money and were the easiest to work with, were new homeowners. I have since developed direct mail campaigns targeting new homeowners with similar avatars and had very successful results.

This process is not an exact science but rather a process of exploration, trial and error. Like all your marketing. With that said, this process takes a lot of the guess work and mistakes out of your marketing campaigns. Defining your target market avatar will help you reduce your waste and increase your ROI. You should have a very specific avatar for every marketing campaign you launch.

An Example of Identifying a Target Market

Here is an example of how you can use the avatar of your clients to increase the ROI of your marketing campaigns. Let's say you want build out your landscape maintenance route for a particular crew. Your goal is to find better customers and reach maximum capacity for a crew so you can drop a few of your annoying and less profitable customers.

You develop a list of your ideal customers and write down everything you know about them. During this process, you discover that 60% of them live in three communities. So, you start your list for your target market with every single-family home in these three communities. As you can see, this list alone is much more targeted than mailing to every home in a zip code.

Next you discover that the average home value for your best customers is $350,000+. So, you would refine your list to only homes of $350,000+ in these three communities. At this point, you should have a really good list that you can develop a marketing campaign around.

Depending on your budget and the number of prospects on your list, you may want to refine it further. The more precise you define your list the more targeted your message (Chapter 8) will be.

For example, if you discover that 40% of your clients work in a specific industry, you can develop a marketing campaign that will focus on your services tied into a message relating to their industry. This level of focus and detail will help with your conversions because you will be able to capture their attention with a precise and personalized message that will speak directly to their needs and wants.

The List, The List, The List

The goal of identifying your target markets is to generate a highly focused and targeted list to which you can market your products or services. As I mentioned in the examples above, you can identify lists of new targets, but there are also other lists you can generate that are both more and less valuable.

Let's look at different target market lists and rank them in relative order of importance and value.

1. <u>Customer Lists</u>: This will always be your most valuable list because the names on this list have bought from you, know you and trust you. You should be communicating to this list with a printed newsletter each month of the year (Yes, I said printed and we will talk more about this in the Chapter 9 about media.).

2. <u>Email Subscriber Lists</u>: This is a list of prospects who have provided their contact information and given you permission to send them email or direct mail, but have not purchased a product or service from you yet.

3. <u>Purchased Direct Mail List</u>: You can purchase a targeted list based on demographics, geography, behavior, budgets, social engagement, profession and almost any other criteria you can think of.

4. <u>Local Publications</u>: These are local community magazines that are distributed to your general local target market.

5. <u>Online Platform Audiences</u>: A list of subscribers to Facebook, LinkedIn, Twitter or any other online platform where you can target content ads to their subscribers.

Now let's look at a few lists you should never use:

1. <u>Purchased Email Lists</u>: This is SPAM. It's annoying. You have no permission to enter their email box and it's illegal. Don't waste your time or ruin your reputation.

2. <u>National or Regional Publications</u>: These magazines are viewed by an audience over too large of a geographic area to be profitable for a local landscape professional.

3. <u>Zip Code Direct Mail List</u>: As mentioned above, this purchased list is too vague. You want to be more focused and targeted towards your audience. Sales people will push this list because of its simplicity, but do not fall into their trap of

irresponsible practices. If it's too easy, it most likely doesn't have much value.

It Costs a Lot to Get This Wrong

When you are building a marketing campaign to grow your landscape business, you must remember the proven Marketing Formula we discussed in the last chapter:

Market + Message + Media + Metrics = Profitable Marketing Campaign

The first step is to clearly identify your target market. If you get this wrong, you will waste a lot of time, money and energy. There is no exception to this rule, only costly consequences if you ignore it. Before you sign up for the next hot marketing fad that comes across your desk, take the time to identify your ideal customer avatar, develop a list of your target market and then you are ready to develop your message which we will discuss in the next chapter.

 CHAPTER 8

Develop Your Marketing Message

Every day you are broadcasting a marketing message to your prospects, customers and public whether you know it or not. The way you answer the phone, the age and condition of the vehicles of your fleet, the look and feel of your website, the layout and structure of your proposals and, most importantly, the words you use in print and verbally.

People are judging your message always. Fairly or not, the message you project has a direct and profound effect on your business, on your ability to attract new business and your ability to increase revenue year after year.

Defining Your Marketing Message

The goal of your marketing message is to differentiate your landscape company from your competitors—both real and imagined—by clearly stating the advantages of doing business with you and inspire your prospect to take action and connect with you. When your message accomplishes this, you are winning. When it doesn't, you are simply another choice amongst many with no tangible or quantifiable identity or advantage.

"So how do I clearly and precisely define my marketing message?"

Funny you should ask.

To clearly and precisely define a marketing message that you can leverage across all applications when marketing your business—both directly or indirectly—you need to develop a statement called your *Unique Selling Proposition* or USP.

You can develop a USP for your entire organization that will drive your business on every level. It can provide a central focus and catalyst for both your day to day activities and your marketing campaigns. I highly recommend that you take the time to develop a USP for your organization.

You can also develop a USP for a specific campaign. You should have a USP for the service you are promoting. The process of developing a USP forces you to get clear on who you are, what benefits to offer and how to most effectively communicate these advantages in your marketing campaign.

Examples of USPs You May Be Familiar With:

The Low-Price Leader: Wal-Mart

The Happiest Place on Earth: Disney

Brewed with the Clear, Cold Water of the Rockies: Coors

Fresh, Hot Pizza Delivered in 30 Minutes or Less, Guaranteed: Domino's

When It Absolutely, Positively Has to Be There Overnight.: FedEx

A Diamond Is Forever: De Beers

The King of Pop: Michael Jackson

The Greatest Show on Earth: Barnum and Bailey Circus

The Ultimate Driving Machine: BMW

The Best a Man Can Get: Gillette

As you can see, each of these USPs clearly describes the unique identity of the business, how they are different and why someone should choose to do business with them. I hope you can also see how these statements can literally affect all aspects of the business from marketing to production. They provide a clear statement everyone can unite behind as the driving force and purpose of the business. When you develop a USP, you are getting much more than a marketing message; you are clarifying your company's identity, your purpose and your vision. When accepted and applied consistently, your USP will have a profound impact on your entire business.

Your USP

When creating your USP you want to avoid statements that do not offer a clear unique advantage over your competitors. For example, a statement that says, "The Best Lawn Care Company in the Tri-County Area" is not a USP. The best is not a competitive advantage; it's not unique no matter how true it might be; it doesn't inspire a customer to act and choose you over all other available options. Neither do statements using "quality", "affordable", "reliable" or any other vague description of benefit. Your USP is a *unique* selling proposition."

Developing a successful USP for your business may take you one hour or one decade. Some companies struggle for years to get a grip on their USP and you may too, but that should not deter you from trying until the light goes off in your head and you know with certainty that you have discovered yours (at least for now).

Message-to-Market Match

When communicating to your target market, the goal is to create a message-to-market match. Meaning, you want to create a message that demonstrates how and why your business is the right choice for your target market's needs and wants.

You want to leverage your USP and create a message focused on the needs and wants of your target market. You then want to apply this message to your marketing campaigns and sale process.

This is the second part of the Marketing Formula:

Market + Message + Media + Metrics = Profitable Marketing Campaign

When you achieve this market-to-message match, you will have a powerful tool that you can use to connect with your target market and generate sales. Without a market-to-message match, you are guessing and hoping for your marketing to work. A very costly strategy if you ask me.

Principles of Direct Marketing: Message

In Chapter 5, I presented *The Principles of Direct Marketing*, which are:

1. *Offers*: You will make an offer or offers on all marketing and advertising materials

2. *Call to Action*: There will be a call to action with a reason to respond immediately

3. *Clear Instructions*: Provide clear instructions

4. *Metrics*: You will track, measure and analyze all results

5. *Follow Up*: Follow up, follow up, follow up

6. *Copywriting*: You will use professional copywriting

7. *Consistency*: You will implement direct marketing campaigns consistently.

Offers, call to action, clear instructions & copywriting are The Principles of Direct Marketing that relate to your marketing message which we will go into more detail here.

Offers

To generate a response, lead and sale, you absolutely must make an offer, or offers, when presenting your marketing message. By presenting offers you can directly quantify your advertisement's results. In contrast, if you look at most of the advertisements landscape companies make, you may notice that they are vague and focus more on promoting their image rather than presenting an offer that will generate a lead or sale.

Avoid being vague with your marketing at all cost. You want to create very specific offers that directly asks someone to do something specific such as request more information, visit a physical location to receive a special offer or even make an immediate purchase. Every marketing message that you create should include an offer or offers. Always.

There are two types of offers you can make. The first is an *offer to purchase*. This could be a *buy one, get one free* offer, a *gift with purchase* offer or something similar. When you present an offer to purchase, you should always insert a hard deadline for the offer. The hard deadline will help you determine the effectiveness of your offer.

There are disadvantages of offers to purchase. The first is they typically sacrifice price and profitability, which can train the customer to only act when there is a discount or special. Another disadvantage is the only people likely to respond are people who are ready to buy now, which eliminates people who may want to purchase in the near future. Finally, when you make an offer to purchase, it can easily be shopped and compared to other similar offers. With that said, at some point a business must make a purchase offer to make a sale.

The second type of offer you can make is called a *lead generation offer*, which reduces marketing losses, instills a marketing culture in your company and allows you to build trust with your prospect. Lead generation offers allow you to connect with people who are considering the services you offer but are reluctant at the time to commit to buying.

Examples of lead generation offers for landscape professionals are:

- Irrigation Offer: information about "how to reduce your monthly water bill and repair costs"

- Maintenance Offer: information about "six most common mistakes landscape maintenance companies make that cost you, the homeowner, every month"

- Design Offer: information about "everything you need to know to hire the perfect landscape designer for your project."

Offer Thresholds

All offers will fall somewhere on a threshold scale from a low threshold offer to a high threshold offer. An example of a low threshold offer is an offer to request more information as mentioned above. These offers do not require the customer to make a purchase decision; they don't even require them to speak to a salesperson. They are low threshold offers that slowly introduce the customer to the marketer.

In contrast, an example of a high threshold offer is a purchase offer to save 20% when you buy now. This offer requires the customer to be ready and willing to buy immediately which is great if they are ready, but a high threshold offer disqualifies many of your prospects at the same time.

A low threshold offer will get a higher response rate, but that doesn't mean you should never use a higher threshold offer. What you can do is offer both at the same time in your marketing message.

Use Irresistible Offers to Put Your Message on Steroids

One of the best ways to increase the effectiveness of your marketing message is to create an irresistible offer to go with it, an offer so good that your target market will pick up the phone and call you ready to do business with you, an offer that inspires your target market to act immediately.

Getting your target market to act is the name of the game. Without action, there is no customer, no sale, no profit, nothing. By presenting an irresistible offer you exponentially increase your chances of motivating your target market to act.

I recently presented an irresistible offer to a country club community of homeowners I was targeting to generate leads for landscape maintenance services. Knowing that summertime is when landscape maintenance companies are required to provide the most services, I also know that is the time when many customers become frustrated with the services being rendered. That provided a great opportunity for me to present an irresistible offer to my target market.

Call to Action

The goal of your marketing is to move the prospect closer to a sale, whether that be an immediate sale or getting them to raise their hand and request more information. To do this you must include a *call to action* in every marketing message that you develop. The call to action is a direct request for the prospect to take a very specific action.

To create a marketing message, develop a marketing campaign and invest in media to deliver your message without a call to action would be poor marketing. Some business owners are shy about a call to action, thinking that it is too pushy. If you are one of these people, get over it or forget about marketing. You must have a call to action if you want to make a sale or engage your prospect.

There must always be a call to action. No exceptions.

Clear Instructions

When developing your marketing message, it's critical that you provide clear instructions as to what exactly you want the prospect to do. You must make it super simple and super easy for the prospect to act. There should be absolutely no confusion as to what they should do next if they want to engage you and your business offer.

I recently received a very "pretty" and expensive direct mail piece from a food subscription business that had great graphics, wonderful images of delicious food, a great headline but a horrible and confusing offer. The design and copywriting of the marketing piece got my attention and held it for a good while but when it came time to under-stand the offer, it was as clear as mud. I read it three times and was completely confused. They lost me. They spent all the time and money to get my attention but lost the sale because I had no idea what the offer was and I was out.

Take the time to make sure the instructions are so clear that a small child would understand. I am not kidding. Provide clear and simple instructions and move the prospect closer to the sale.

Professional Copywriting

As you can see there are many parts and pieces of creating a great message to reach your target market, but having professional copywriting by far can have the most impact on your ROI. I will take professional copywriting over gorgeous graphics and images in my marketing pieces any day.

It's the words that move people to take immediate action, not the images or graphics. Understanding the principles of quality and professional copywriting takes effort and most likely your graphic artist does not have a clue about professional copywriting. Don't rely on your graphic artist or media sales rep to write your copy for your next marketing piece. To get the most out of the media you must have professional copywriting that connects your message with your market.

This topic is way too large to cover in this book but I highly recommend that you understand the fundamentals of professional copywriting and/or find a copywriter to assist you when developing your marketing message. It will pay off many times over and once you learn it, you will be able to leverage it forever.

This is a very important step in *creating your own landscape economy* because when you can leverage professional copywriting in your marketing messages, you can generate quality customers and projects almost on demand.

 CHAPTER 9

Media. How to Connect with Your Market.

Media, when chosen correctly, is the link between your message and your market. It's the portal that brings your message to your market. Nothing more, nothing less.

A big mistake landscape professionals, and most small business owners, make is they start their marketing campaign by committing to a media source. This typically happens because they see their competitor using it or they hear a buzz about a new media platform.

Starting your marketing campaign by selecting your media before you identify your target market or develop your message is a big mistake. The media alone will not convince quality customers to call you for your services. You need to slow down and start by identifying your target market & message and before you spend a dime on any media.

Shiny Object Media Mistakes

Along with the rise of the Internet and social media as a marketing media over the past two decades has come a significant amount of wasted time and money. When a buzz about a new Internet platform, from Google to LinkedIn to Facebook to SnapChat, etc. hits the streets, small business owners, including landscape companies, fall victim to the new shiny object syndrome.

Many business owners feel like they must immediately invest marketing dollars into these platforms or they will be missing out on an opportunity. They find the first person who knows how to speak Facebook, SnapChat or whatever, and they start handing over money without having a clue of what they are doing. I would love to know how much marketing dollars has been wasted over the past two decades because of the hype.

What Media Does Your Target Market Respond To?

All media has value to some businesses and some target markets, but not all media works for all businesses and all target markets. The name of the game is to find the media that your target market responds to. Believe it or not, the yellow pages still work for some businesses and some target markets. Seniors still use the yellow pages, especially seniors who don't like computers, and while this audience is getting smaller by the year, there are still some businesses that are benefiting from their yellow pages ads.

By taking the time to first identify your target market and develop your marketing message you can then more accurately select the media that will work best for your business. I am a big fan of direct mail as a media for landscape professionals because you can select your target market based on home location, home value, income and other relevant information. With direct mail, you can capture the attention of your target market without interruption and effectively present your irresistible offer.

The most important aspect of using direct mail as a media source is the selection and creation of your mailing list. You need to make sure you are presenting your message to the right target market, and you do that by curating a mailing list that represents your ideal customer. There is no reason for a landscaper to market their residential maintenance services to multi-story condominium owners.

This holds true for all media. I recently had a saleswoman call me about advertising in an exclusive 'high-end" magazine that was mailed to thousands of million dollar and multi-million dollar homes. Being that we offer landscape architecture design-build services, on the surface this magazine sounded like a great opportunity to present our message to a very exclusive audience.

As I asked a few questions I learned that this magazine would be delivered to our tri-county area that covers over 75 miles north to south. This immediately disqualified this media for our marketing plan because the area was just too large. Most of the audience would be outside our service area and thus most likely the campaign would not be successful. Of course, there is an outside chance that we would attract a customer within our target market and turn a profit on the campaign, but that was a risk I was not willing to take. I prefer to be very diligent about every dollar we spend on marketing and provide the best possible ROI.

Media Options Are Infinite

There are an infinite number of media options available to market your landscape business. Everything from direct mail to billboards to Facebook to Google to calendars to sports bottles to flying banners at sporting events and beyond. Each of these media outlets have the potential to produce a positive ROI for a business somewhere.

The question is, is this media the right media to connect your message with your target market? It's your responsibility to properly test the media outlets. You should go to great lengths to determine the ROI from each media outlet you invest in. Otherwise, you are guessing, and guessing is no way to spend hard earned money on your marketing campaigns.

With that said, I would like to list media outlets that when used properly, can work well for landscape companies. Keep in mind this list is just suggestions from my experiences. Whether they produce a positive ROI for you and your company is determined by the quality of your campaign. How well you choose your target market and develop your message.

The following are a few media options you should consider when marketing your landscape company:

- Direct Mail
  - Newsletter
  - Postcards
  - Sales Letters

- Digital Media
  - Social Media: Sponsored Posts
    - I prefer Facebook but you may want to test other platforms as well.
  - Google: Pay-per-click Campaigns
  - Re-Marketing Campaigns
  - Email; newsletters, specials & promotions
  - Content Marketing; blog syndication

- Print Advertising
  - Magazines
  - Newspapers
  - Community Newsletters

Remember, Direct Response Is the Goal

No matter which media source you select and test, remember the goal is to generate a direct response from your marketing piece. You want to use the media to connect your message with the right market and generate a direct response. That is the name of the game.

Don't get confused, overwhelmed or overhyped by any one media source. They should all be placed on a trial period when you first implement them. If they cannot deliver results, then tweak the campaign and test again, or if it appears to be a complete loser move on.

The media must prove itself and provide profitable results for your business. Be open-minded to the media you select and use the media that proves it works for you and your business, not what you hear about online or see your competitors using. Find the media that works for you and rinse and repeat it until it no longer works.

An Old Secret Weapon

I am going to share with you a very successful media platform that you can use to engage your customers, increase retention rates, increase upsells, increase repeat business, increase referrals and increase sales year after year.

Printed Newsletters.

Yes, I said it. Printed Newsletters.

In an era of digital everything and automated everything, the printed newsletter is a secret weapon that can add consistent and predictable revenue to your business year after year. There is a learning curve to getting it going and you must commit the time each month, but when done correctly, and when you track your results you will quickly see how valuable it is. Not to mention it's a very cheap media platform, much cheaper than many Google or other direct mail options, but can produce a positive ROI.

If you are wondering whether you can just send an email newsletter the answer is yes, but you will not generate as much of a return because not as many people will read your email newsletter as your printed newsletter that is mailed to them. I recommend sending both if you really want to *create your own landscape economy.*

 CHAPTER 10

Metrics: Keeping Score.

Understanding your marketing campaign metrics is the final component of the marketing formula. Your marketing metrics is the data, or analytics, that you collect regarding your marketing campaign performance so you can determine if your campaign was a success or not.

Knowing your metrics is essential if you are going to *create your own landscape economy* because it's your metrics that tell you what is working, what is not working and what steps to take next. If your campaign is working you obviously want to run the campaign again and possibly expand it. If your campaign is not working, then you don't want to just abandon it and forget about it. You want to leverage your experience and see if you can determine why the campaign is not working. Was it your headline? Was it your offer? Was it the media platform? By digging deep into your metrics and asking a lot of questions, you can learn a lot about your business, your target market and your marketing campaigns.

Your Marketing Must Be Accountable for Its Existence

Far too many landscape companies leave their marketing and sales to happenstance. They don't track and thoroughly analyze their numbers. For whatever reason, they simply do not keep track of the money they spend on marketing and determine whether they are getting a positive return on investment. Many companies get in a routine of placing the same ads with the same media and just figure if the work is coming in, there is no reason to quantify where it is coming from.

When *creating your own landscape economy*, this thinking is simply not good enough. You must be able to quantify your metrics from every campaign, every customer, every product, every service and much more. Knowing your numbers is critical to *creating your own landscape economy* because when the economy shifts or competition tightens you will know how to respond. You will have the analytics to adjust and continue to prosper, which is the purpose of *creating your own landscape economy.*

You Can't Compete Unless You Are Keeping Score

The following numbers, when collected, analyzed and applied to your future marketing and sales activities, will allow you to effectively compete in any business environment or condition. Having a true understanding of these numbers will provide you a powerful competitive advantage that most, if not all, of your competitors will not have. Knowing these numbers will empower you and your business to new and amazing heights.

Cost Per Lead = CPL

Cost Per Sale = CPS

Average Transaction Value = ATV

Revenue Per Lead = RPL

Lifetime Customer Value = LCV, this is especially important in the landscape industry because of the opportunities of repeat business, which can change your campaign ROI very easily

Closing Rate = CR, how many leads converted into sales over a specific period: month, quarter, year

Average Length of Transaction = ALT, the average amount of time a sale takes from when it enters the pipeline until it closes

Pipeline = Current leads, proposals, deals in the pipeline and their value

Lead Generation Rate: The amount of leads generated per day, week, month, quarter and year versus same period the previous year

Revenue Per Month: What was your gross revenue for the month?

Product & Service Close Rates: Which products and services have the best close rates? Why?

Campaign Metrics: Which campaigns are working best? Why?

Media Metrics: Which media is producing the most ROI? Why?

Create a spreadsheet and start tracking these numbers. As you track and analyze them, you will gain tremendous insight into what's working and what's not working. Then you adjust and push forward. There is power in knowing your numbers. You will begin to make different decisions and produce better results. While not every marketing & sales campaign will be a home run, they will give you insights and power to gain control of your business and *create your own landscape economy.*

IMPORTANT NOTE: It only works if you act and stay focused on the process.

How to Create Your Own Landscape Economy

 CHAPTER 11

Sales Machine. You Must Have One That Works Really Really Well!

You have successfully created the marketing portion of your marketing & sales machine. Now it is time to create the sales portion of the machine. This is the fun part. This is where all the hard work and investment of time, energy and money produces a result. Until now you have been working on experience, belief and faith that your actions will result in sales which will grow your business.

But there is still a lot of very important work to do. You must close the sale and that is never guaranteed. I am sure you have had the experience of taking a call from a customer, scheduling an initial consultation, going to the meeting, creating great rapport with the customer, providing them a proposal, feeling almost certain that you will get the project and then silence. You never hear from them again or if you do, they tell you they have "gone with someone else."

What? How did that happen?

Well there are many reasons a client chooses another landscape company and you will never close 100% of your leads, but there are very specific actions you can take when building your sales machine to increase your conversion rate and close more sales.

There Is a Fuzzy Line Between Your Marketing Campaign and Your Sales Process

A good sales process is intertwined with your marketing campaign. It starts well before you submit your proposal. It starts during the marketing campaign where you are either introducing yourself to a prospect or reconnecting with an existing customer. During your marketing campaign your goal is to get the prospect to act and contact you for your services or more information. At the same time, you are building trust and rapport that will be used during the sales process.

When you invest time to understand the needs and wants of your target market and develop a very specific message to reach them, you are also building trust with your prospect. You are speaking to their needs and wants. You are answering the W.I.I.F.M (what's in it for me) question every consumer is asking before they act. These are the first steps of any good sales process.

Advanced Sales Tip: Hello! Could Be the Most Important Word You Speak.

For all our marketing campaigns, we use phone tracking numbers to help improve our metrics. One of the very helpful features of our phone tracking numbers is a *call whisper*. This is a short voice message that is spoken into your phone before the call is transferred to you. We usually script a call whisper that says something like "This is a call from your fall marketing postcard campaign."

The benefit of applying this technology is that we can quickly prepare our greeting and tone to make a positive first impression for the caller. We know they are a hot lead calling in response to our marketing campaign, and we can leverage this information to set the tone for the phone call and the entire sales process.

How we say "Hello!" can literally be the most important word we speak during the entire sales process. Now, I know that is a bold statement but think about it, if an upscale customer is responding to your direct mail piece and is interested in discussing a large landscape design-build project worth 10's of thousands of dollars, how you handle the first phone call will have an immediate and lasting impact on the entire sales process. If you answer the call with a low energy monotone, it's only natural that the prospect is going to feel that and react to it.

Remember, new customers do not trust you. They are interviewing you and most likely very skeptical of contractors in general so something as simple as starting the phone call with a high energy, passionate and thoughtful greeting will make a positive impact in the early stages of the sales process.

Now you might be thinking, *Matt, that is ridiculous. I am not going to lose a sale because I did not inject enough passion in the way I say hello.* While you might be right, the point I am trying to make is that your sales process starts from the very first impression you make with the prospect, and if using a call whisper can help you bring more passion and focus to the phone call, it will increase your chances to close the sale. Admittedly this will be hard to quantify, but

I know from personal experience that when I bring passion and energy to my customers, they typically respond in kind and it leads to a more fruitful relationship.

Call scripts for your incoming sales calls implementing a call whisper is a great way get ready for the call. It's another simple but very effective competitive advantage I am sure your competition is not using. The question is, will you?

Sales Don't Just Happen

The thing about sales systems is that there is not a one size fits all system for every landscape company or every salesperson. Anybody that tells you otherwise is mistaken. A sales system must be developed by each company and each salesperson to work for their culture, style, personality and working environment. It's not so important how your sales system works as much as it is that you have a sales system that works *for you*, because sales don't just happen.

While it's true that if you run effective marketing campaigns you are going to get enough calls that you will make some sales naturally without much effort. You will connect with like-minded customers who are a good fit for you and your company, and you will make a few sales with minimal effort. This is also how most everybody else is playing the game, which is a major advantage for you when you create your custom sales system.

To close more sales and beat your competition with your superior sales system, you need to break down every point of contact with the prospect and identify ways you can add value to the customer and their experience during the sales process. To do this, ask how can you leverage every point of contact from the first phone call, to the confirmation email, to the initial consultation, to the follow-up emails, to the format of your proposal, to the contract terms, to the follow-up system and so on, to create a competitive advantage for your business and thus a winning sales process.

Again, the only magic formula for this process is the one you create, but there is a process to creating your sales system and that is by breaking down every touch point of communication and adding value and building trust and rapport with your prospect. Simply showing up, asking a couple questions and offering a low-price proposal is not a sales system. That is a recipe for struggle and frustration.

Creating a sales system that addresses every single point of contact and thinks about how to provide value and a pleasant experience for the prospect is a sales system that will help you *create your own landscape economy*. When you create your version of this rock-solid sales system, you will be guaranteed to beat out your competition for those competitive proposals. When done correctly, you will begin to win bids even if your price is not the lowest because you have built so much trust and rapport. Having a rock-solid sales system is a competitive advantage you can quantify with your bottom line year after year.

Understanding Personalities and Tendencies

If you study personality indexes, you will learn that there are different personality types. It can be very useful to understand your personality type and how to identify the personality of your prospect so you will have a strategy of engagement during the sales process.

If your prospect has a Dominant personality, they will typically lead the meeting, tell you what they want and ask for a proposal. If your prospect has a very Social or Promoter type personality, they may ask more questions and be more interested in your ideas. The point here is that by understanding your personality and the personality of your prospect you can better serve the needs and wants of your prospect.

A sure-fire way to kill a deal is to give the prospect exactly what they are *not* looking for. For example, say a prospect calls you and requests a meeting to discuss landscaping their backyard. From your initial phone conversation, it is clear they know what they want; they have done their research and they have a Dominant personality type. But during the initial consultation, wanting to demonstrate your knowledge and experience, you take over the meeting from the beginning. You start talking ideas and telling them what you think and how their project should look, etc. You are in effect shooting yourself in the foot because you are not allowing the customer to do what comes naturally them and control the meeting and environment. Your presentation is in direct conflict to the personality of your prospect and thus, you are hurting your chances of closing the sale because you are not building trust and rapport.

In this situation, if you recognize that you are dealing with a Dominant personality, you want to spend more time listening, ask very direct and specific questions, listen to their answers and offer suggestions and recommendations as necessary. Be conscious of their needs and personality type and reflect it back to them. They don't want to be dominated, but they don't like sheepish, weak and indecisive personalities either. Be confident, firm and passionate, and you will build trust and rapport and increase your chances of closing the sale.

Taking the time to study Personality Index programs and learning about your personality will equip you with a great tool you can use to improve your sales machine and help you close more sales. Invest the time and this skill, and it will serve you for the rest of your life.

Estimating Is Not Guesswork

The preparation and presentation of your estimate should be a very exact and precise science. A formula that accounts for your cost of goods, labor, general & administrative overhead and profit. There are many ways to construct an estimate, but if your method does not carefully account for all of these components, then your estimating method is faulty.

This subject is much too large to go in depth here, but much too important not to mention. I highly recommend that you evaluate your estimating system and if you are not accounting for cost of goods, labor, overhead and profit, I suggest that you spend whatever time necessary to find the estimating system that works best for you.

With that said, I am going to tell you one estimating system that I do not recommend using, and that is the simple multiplier method. This is when you take the cost of your materials and simply multiply them by 2, 3, 1.8, 2.3 or any other random number you guess to use. This is one of the most common methods but also one of the worst because it does not accurately account for your overhead, your labor and your profit. It assumes that the cost of materials multiplied will cover these items. If you are using this method, please stop.

Estimating is a crucial part of *creating your own landscape economy*. If you are not in control of your numbers, then you really don't know how to run your business. In effect, you have a very expensive hobby. This industry demands way too much from us to treat it as a hobby. Learn your numbers and learn how to estimate correctly, and you will be well on your way to *creating your own landscape economy.*

Personalize Your Sales Machine and Close More Sales

As I have said many times in this book, each of these processes and systems must be developed and personalized to serve your personality, your business model and your target market. There is never a one size fits all solution to marketing & sales. Yes, there are proven tactics that work when specific formulas are implemented, i.e. the marketing formula, but even that must be personalized by the user.

I am reinforcing this fact because I don't want you to get bogged down in the details of trying to replicate a sales system step by step that works for me or anyone else. Adopt the ideas, concepts and even formulas, but know that it's your application, testing and adjusting that will result in your personalized sales machine. It's the process of taking the concepts and ideas and implementing them and building on them that will result in an amazingly productive and profitable sales machine that will transform your business.

Need Help Reaching Your Business Goals?

The Strategic Landscaper Coaching Program can help you define your goals, construct a roadmap to achieve them and mentor you along the way. Matt Hudson accepts a limited number of clients each year for personalized one on one coaching.

APPLY AT:

StrategicLandscaper.Com/Coaching

Strategic Landscaper Sales System Example

The following is an example of a sales system that breaks down each touch point with a customer during the sales process and provides value to the customer's experience, which results in building trust and rapport and significantly increases the chance of closing the sale.

If you are going to *create your own landscape economy*, you must first create, implement, test and continually adjust your sales system because it's your sales system that is the final phase of your marketing & sales machine and ultimately quantifies your results. An amazing marketing machine with a poor sales machine is doomed for failure because they are working against each other. They must work congruently, not separately. It takes discipline, focus and commitment to create a successful marketing & sales machine, but I know you can do it!

1. *Prospect Reads Media Ad*: by implementing The Principles of Direct Marketing, you increase the chance of generating a target lead who is interested in your services.

2. *Initial Phone Call*: using a call whisper and initial call script to position yourself and your business as offering quality services and exceptional customer care.

3. *Confirmation Email*: during the initial phone call, set an appointment, capture the prospect's contact information including email address and send them an appointment confirmation email. In this email, include the date and time of the appointment as well as additional information about the services they are requesting. This is a great opportunity to build trust and position your business as a leader.

4. *Appointment Confirmation Phone Call*: The day of the appointment, a few hours prior, call the prospect to confirm the appointment time. No selling, just a courtesy reminder call.

5. *Running Late Phone Call*: I have a policy that if I am running more than 3 minutes late to an appointment, I call the prospect and tell them I am on my way and running just a couple minutes late. I have found that this builds trust and rapport as well because it demonstrates respect and consideration for the prospect's time. Think about how many of your competitors won't bother calling or even showing up. Who do you think they will hire if timing and respect are the determining factors?

6. *Initial Consultation Objectives*: During your initial consultation, you need to understand that this is your first person to person meeting and your best chance to make a first impression. You should have a strategy to make the most of this appointment and set the table for the remaining part of the sales process as well as closing the sale. The following is a list of general objectives to accomplish during your initial consultation:

a. Warm and open greeting.

b. Position your business with a flyer or brochure—a takeaway pamphlet of some kind that they can read after you leave. Never just give a business card; that is a wasted opportunity.

c. Ask open-ended questions.

d. Listen.

e. Listen.

f. Listen.

g. Give confident and clear answers, ideas, solutions. This is your opportunity to position yourself as an expert and separate yourself from the competition. If you don't know the answer, that is okay. But be honest and tell them you will look into it and get back to them. Always keep your word and get back to them in the timeframe promised.

h. Establish clear next steps. This is where you get to influence the process. Are you going to provide an email proposal, schedule another meeting, etc.? Set clear expectations and timeline before leaving the meeting.

7. *Same Day Follow-up Email.*

8. *Fulfill Established Expectations*: At this point in the sales process, the timeline, expectations and responsibilities will vary depending on the client's needs, the project, etc. The most important thing to do is to keep your word! Be timely, respectful and meet or exceed their expectations, whether it is getting them a proposal the next day or designing a landscape within two weeks. Do as you promise or better! That's my lecture on that. If you fail to keep your word, you will destroy all trust and rapport that you have spent so much time and energy creating. It's such a waste and it happens all the time, which can be a competitive advantage for you if you leverage it.

9. *Submit Proposal*: If in person present proposal and shut up. Wait for feedback. If over email call them to let them know you sent it and ask them to call you after they review it.

10. *Follow Up*: Again your follow-up process will need to be customized for your personality type, business model and target market. You must follow-up and nurture the prospect until they agree to a contract or tell you to stop contacting them. Just because they don't buy on this proposal doesn't mean they won't buy from you in the future. *See Chapter 13: Following Up for more information.*

 CHAPTER 12

Seasonal Campaigns

By far the most effective marketing is the most precise marketing. The more accurate and precise the information you can gather about your target market, details you develop in your marketing message and the metrics about your media and campaigns, the higher your ROI will be.

Another important factor to consider when developing and implementing your marketing campaign is timing. This is especially important for landscape companies because of the seasonal nature of our industry. The seasonality provides a degree of predictability and thus a real competitive advantage to you as a marketer if you seize it.

I liken it to a competitive season for a football team. Knowing the season's schedule allows a team to plan for the season year-round. While the games may be played in Fall and early Winter, teams train and plan for those games all year. They know what opponent is coming and they know their team so they work year-round to put themselves in the best position to win.

The seasonality of the landscape industry is very similar. Here in South Florida, where I live and work, our peak season is from January 1 to April 31. This is when the snowbirds come south and our population doubles, resulting in a lot of business to be had. In other regions, the peak months are Spring and Fall.

Regardless of where you live or when your peak season is, you can plan for all seasons of the year to attract new customers and leverage your existing customers for repeat business. By incorporating these seasonal demands into your marketing & sales machine, you are able to provide a more precise marketing message and irresistible offer which in turn will increase your ROI.

Seasonal Marketing Campaigns

It's easiest to simply break your marketing plan into the four seasons of the year: Winter, Spring, Summer and Fall. From here you want to design, build and implement campaigns for each season. This is a great time to get your marketing message laser tight because you can speak about the seasonal needs and wants of your target market.

If spring cleanups are a big part of your business, you can design, build and implement marketing campaigns specifically timed to meet the demand for spring cleanups. Knowing this demand is consistent every year, you should start your campaign one to two months before the services are needed. Offer an early bird special for those who sign up and send a deposit in now. This is a great way to attract new customers and increase your cash flow during the slow months.

If you offer irrigation maintenance services, the hotter summer months are going to be your peak season. Knowing this in advance, you can design, build and implement marketing campaigns to sign up new monthly irrigation maintenance contracts. Again, you can offer this service in advance of the seasonal demand, which will allow you to schedule your services in advance.

There is nothing like being booked solid for an entire season before it even starts. *That's creating your own landscape economy!*

The seasonal marketing campaign options are literally endless. The only limit is your imagination and commitment to implementing them. Not leveraging the seasonality of our industry is simply foolish.

To send out a branding type direct mail piece during any season without speaking the about the seasonal demands is leaves opportunity on the table. Sure, you will get a few calls because of the overwhelming demand of the season, but you won't be maximizing the opportunity and you definitely won't be *creating your own landscape economy.*

Different Types of Seasonal Marketing Campaigns

When designing your seasonal marketing campaigns there are a variety of options to consider. You can design a campaign focusing on your existing customers and promoting seasonal services they have used in the past but need you to remind them that it is time to schedule the services again. You can create a campaign for your existing customers that introduces a new product or service that you want to promote and provides a seasonal special or incentive to act now and save.

These campaigns are great for the off seasons, when you are not as busy and need to generate business. An example might be landscape lighting system installation in the winter months. You can install lighting year-round, and it's a great opportunity to create a win-win offer for your clients while keeping your crews busy making money in the slow months.

Low threshold lead generation campaigns are great seasonal campaigns as well. For this type of campaign, you would create a free informational resource like a free report or guide that is related to the current or upcoming season and use it to capture the name and email address of people interested in your services. An example would be something like, "How to Have the Most Attractive Flowering & Fragrant Spring Landscape in Your Community." This would attract customers who care about their landscape and would be a potential customer for you. Once they give you their name and email address, they are entered into your sales funnel and off you go.

As you can see, your imagination is your only limitation

when it comes to designing seasonal marketing campaigns for your landscape business. The important thing to remember is to plan your seasonal campaigns well in advance, because you don't want to be mailing a Spring campaign in Summer. Seasonal campaigns are very strategic and can become a real competitive advantage for your business and help you *create your own landscape economy.*

 CHAPTER 13

Following Up: There Is a Ton of Money Waiting For You

Details, details, details. That is where many real and lasting profits are found when running a landscape company. In the case of *creating your own landscape economy*, many extra profits are determined by how well you follow up on your marketing leads.

A typical landscape professional will spend thousands of dollars marketing their company on any campaign, and if the campaign produces a profit, they consider it a success and move on the next campaign.

But wait! There is more!

Let's say you invest $2,500 on a seasonal direct mail campaign and you generate 10 inbound phone calls. From the

10 calls, you generate two sales that create $35,000 in sales at a 15% net profit margin, resulting in a net cash profit of $5,250. You have just doubled your investment, which is fantastic and probably the reason most landscape professionals do not look any further and move on to the next marketing campaign.

This is where the details are missed and the extra profits remain to be discovered. There are 8 more inbound phone calls that should be followed up on. They may not be ready to buy at that very moment, but who's to say they will not buy in the future or buy another service they don't even know you provide? Understanding the real value of following up is where many extra profits await. It's in the detail of following up that you can increase your ROI from your marketing campaign many times over.

Make It Possible to Follow Up

To follow up with your prospects, you must always collect their contact information. In the landscape industry, this is typically easy because in most situations, you will meet the prospect at their home for a consultation. When they first call you, capture as much information as possible: name, address, phone number and email address. Then immediately send them an email with general information about your appointment, your company, etc. This will establish an acceptance of receiving information from you, which will help later when you need to follow up.

Create a Follow Up System for Every Scenario

There is no one size fits all follow up system. You need to customize your follow up system for each scenario so that it makes sense and provides you the best opportunity to connect with the prospect. For example, if you recently completed a new landscape installation for a new, satisfied customer, you should immediately follow up with them as part of your system. This system might include multiple touch points laid out over the next couple weeks such as phone calls, emails, site visits, etc. When the project is fresh in their mind, and yours, is the time to start the follow up process. Don't fall off the face of the earth chasing the next project and forget the many opportunities. You must follow up and sell them additional products or services. Keep the relationship alive and well.

Another example of a completely different follow up system is following up on referrals. When a customer says they told their neighbor about you and "they should be calling you," you should immediately request their contact information and put them into a referral follow up system. The timing, frequency and messaging of the referral follow up system will differ from the new customer follow up system, but there are real opportunities and profits to be made in each system.

Remember: There Must Be Offers

Your follow up campaigns will have different strategies but at some point in the process, you should offer your products and services. Depending on the marketing campaign, you might want to offer the same offer you have previously submitted, you might want to add a deadline, you might want to send them a sequence of notices culminating with a final notice, or you might want to change the offer entirely in lieu of a new product or service.

How your follow up campaign looks and functions will vary from scenario to scenario, but the important takeaway is that you include an offer or offers to generate more business. There are literally millions of dollars of business to be had in following up with your customers over the life of your business. Take the time and effort to follow up because it's a very important component of *creating your own land-scape economy.*

How to Create Your Own Landscape Economy

 CHAPTER 14

Get Clear. It's About Service.

If you want to *create your own landscape economy,* the final piece of the system is to provide world class, best in class, no excuses, exceptional, detail oriented, on-time, professional service all the time. No exceptions. You must be so good that your customers cannot and will not live without you. This is the secret weapon. This is your ace in the hole.

When you are this good, when you are so revered by your customers you have reached the service mountain top. I'm not talking about your customers liking you and paying their bill on time each month. I'm talking about your customers talking about how great you are at their next dinner party. I'm talking about your customers referring you to their friends and family without your request. I'm talking about getting calls from referrals who are so excited to meet with you that you can feel their excitement over the phone. This can only happen when you provide the best service in the entire world.

It's Simple but by No Means Easy

To achieve this level of service, you must want to be the best. You must know what being the best looks like, and you must be willing to sacrifice to achieve it. This level of service and recognition does not happen by accident, and it does not happen by just "doing a good job." It requires intense focus, commitment and an ability to think like your customer and for your customer. It's about details. It's about employee training and accountability. It's about timely communication. It's about preventative care. It's about doing what doesn't have to be done because it's the right thing to do.

This level of service cannot be argued with. When it is consistently delivered over an extended period, you gain authority and invaluable trust with your client. They respect and appreciate you, your business and your employees. And if they don't, you have considerable leverage to work for someone else who does appreciate and respect you.

You see 95%+ of the businesses out there do not come close to offering this level of service. It's either not in their DNA, or their business is so unorganized they don't have the mental focus, manpower or priority to deliver this level of service. Which is great news for you! It's an opportunity that is so readily available if you just make it a priority.

You can't fake this level of service achievement. It must be earned and if you think you have earned it, ask yourself this one question: if I raised my prices by 15% tomorrow, how many of my customers would keep me? If the answer is less than 50%, you are not close to this level of services achievement. Of course, if you are a commercial installation contractor your percentages would be different, but even in B2B there are opportunities to command higher prices because your services are so much inferior to your competitor's.

What World Class Landscaping Service Looks Like

This level of service starts with your marketing and your focused message because this is where you are considering the needs and wants of your target market. You are thinking about what would make them want to do business with you.

It's like dating; when you are first attracted to someone, you spend time thinking about them. You go out of your way to make sure they are happy. You care what they think and feel about you. This level of focus on the client must never dull, must never disappear over the course of time.

It should increase as you get to know your customer. When you learn their birthday, you add it to your CRM and schedule a card to be sent to them every year forever. This will cost you $3/year but can build enormous amounts of good will. When you learn that they are dealing with a death in the family, you send flowers with a nice note expressing your condolences. When you notice that their irrigation head is broken you fix it and send them a note that says it's done before they have to discover it and call you.

You send them a printed monthly newsletter every month with informative, helpful and personalized information they will enjoy. You occasionally call them just to check in, say hello and see if there is anything you can do for them. If your area experiences a large storm that causes flooding or wind damage, you stop by to check the property and send them a quick note with your observations and recommendations. You send an email every week to 10 days touching base, providing information, making new offers with special discounts for existing customers only.

For Thanksgiving, you send them a card and small gift saying thank you for their business. You make sure that every time you service their property, when you leave it looks 100% amazing! You train your employees to think like you, think like your customers. You train your employees to be courteous, helpful and kind to their customers always, because it's the right thing to do, not because they must.

As you get to know your customers over the years, it should be a personal mission to discover what makes them tick and make sure they know you understand them, care about them and have their back always. When you do this, you will have a customer for life, you will have leverage, you will be able to raise your prices beyond anything you thought was possible. You will only work for the best customers. You will at least double your income, and your career will never be the same.

Service Is the Glue That Binds

At this point you have the entire recipe to *create your own landscape economy*. you have the formula to transform your business and your life forever. It's simple but not always easy, but when you build these systems and they become automatic over the course of time you will find that it is much easier and enjoyable to best the best than it is to struggle year after year.

By starting at the beginning and committing to building your own Marketing & Sales Machine as the engine that will drive your independence you will be on the right track. When you take the time to establish your annual budget and build a marketing plan that works within your means year after year you will have a road map and time line for *creating your own landscape economy.*

As you study direct marketing, you will significantly increase the effectiveness of your campaigns and your ROI for every marketing dollar you invest. The ability to implement these methods of marketing are crucial to your ability to scale and gain control over your working environment. By spending time and investing money to clearly identify and attract your ideal customers, you will find that you can charge more money and enjoy working with your customers. You can fire the customers who are a pain in the neck and don't pay the best.

As you continue to define your target market, you will have the insights to develop messages that speak to their needs and wants, which in turn will improve your communication and improve your close rates and profits. As you test different media throughout the year with your seasonal campaigns, you will discover which media your target market is responding to. Then you can scale your investment with that media and ride that train as far as it will take you if the metrics prove successful.

At this point, you find yourself with a system that consistently attracts the best customers and provides enough leads so you can keep your crews busy and profitable year-round. The glue that binds this process and ensures that you *create your own landscape economy*, where you can work only for the best customers, raise your prices and double your income is providing world class service every day and always.

When you reach this level of service, you will be unstoppable. If you fail to do this, you will see an increase in business and might confuse it as *creating your own landscape economy*, but as you try to raise your prices and your customers jump ship, you will know that you have not reached the service mountain top. It's the world class service that is the glue to this system. You are in the service industry; never forget that. Your job is to provide value and solve problems for people. It just so happens that you do this with landscaping services.

Commit to the Process

As this book comes to an end, I'd like to leave you with a few words of encouragement and perspective. Over the hundreds of business and self-improvement books that I have read, many times I read the last page and I am excited—pumped to get to work, make the changes and experience the results. Sometimes the results come easy; other times they are elusive.

The information provided in this book works. I know because I have used it and experienced the results in my businesses over the years. But I want to be very clear: while it may be simple, it will not be easy. To *create your own landscape economy*, you must commit to a process that will take you there. This process is not supposed to be easy. If it was, everybody would be doing it. I could use many other clichés here but I think you get the point.

Don't get me wrong; this process can be fun. You can enjoy yourself along the way, but you must be willing to commit to the process and focus on your goal of *creating your own landscape economy*. You must be willing to find the time to learn new skills, implement new marketing & sales strategies, train your employees to understand and implement your vision every day and take inventory of your successes along the way.

Commit to the process. Trust yourself. As a landscape entrepreneur, you have an amazing opportunity to create an extraordinary business, career and life for you and your employees. It's simply a matter of having a vision and committing to the process.

Start now and best of luck!

 CHAPTER 15

The Missing Pieces

This final chapter could have been the first chapter of this book, but I have elected to move it to the end because what I am going to share with you here is a shift in focus and requires an open mind. Had I covered this information in the beginning, it would have distributed the sequential flow and process outlined to *create your own landscape economy*. With that said, before you apply anything you learn from this book, I want you to first address the items I cover here because if you ignore these insights, your results will be significantly impacted.

The longer I live the more I realize just how short and precious life is. I think it's natural to gain this perspective as you get older. I am now 42 and I recognize that my youth is gone. My early adult life is over and I am entering the prime of my professional career. As a lifelong landscape entrepreneur, I have spent many years grinding away at 50- and 60-hour work weeks, which for the most part have paid off for me very well. I have gained a wealth of knowledge and experience, and this hard work ethic has provided the comfortable and secure life I have today. All in all, I have no major regrets about my career and professional choices to date.

At the same time, I am learning that being a landscape professional does not have to be difficult, frustrating or painful. It can be fun, prosperous and exciting. Of course, there are going to be challenging days, weeks, months and even years, but all in all when you have the correct information, knowledge, vision and focus, you can build an amazing business that supports your preferred lifestyle and goals. Again, it's not always going to be easy and it will not happen overnight, but it is absolutely realistic and feasible to have a wonderfully productive, profitable and rewarding landscape career from day one.

I want to take a minute to speak directly to a few topics and suggestions that are either intentionally or unintention- ally void from most business strategy books and resources. These are the parts of any success formula that must be addressed, but since they are often harder to quantify, people are reluctant to acknowledge or include them in their business strategy. But I can honestly attest that without applying some of these success principles to any strategy, the end results will be disappointing. Some of the following ideas and concepts may seem simple and obvious while others may seem odd or unorthodox. Regardless, they are all relevant and I urge you to consider how you can apply them to your life so you can generate lasting success for you and your family.

You Must Know What You Want

The concept of *creating your own landscape economy* is, at its core, gaining control of your business, reaching your goals and creating a lifestyle that provides the security, peace of mind and the opportunities you desire. Before this is ever going to be possible for you, you must first clearly define exactly what it is that you want. What lifestyle do you want to live and how can your business support that for you?

You may be perfectly content with a business that is 100% cash positive, with a recurring net profit of $75,000 and a piece of land paid for as your long-term investment. This might be your definition of success and security. Or you might want to build a $5 million company that has two offices and 50 employees that generates $500k in net profits for you per year.

The point is the choice is yours, but the first step to accomplishing anything of real value is to clearly define what it is that you desire. Write out your goals in any and all areas of your life. Define them as best you can. State how much and by when. Paint a clear picture of what it is that you want and spend a consistent amount of time focusing on your goals and how you plan to achieve them.

It's this second step of consistently focusing on your goals that will help guide you towards achieving your goals. Simply writing your goals down on January 1st of every year and not looking at them until a year later will not help you at all. Spend time and energy to consistently think about your goals and what your next step is going to be to achieve them. Trust yourself and you will find the way.

Build Your Business to Match Your Goals

Once you know what you to achieve, build your business to match. If you only want to work four days a week, you can do that. If you want to work six days a week for five years, build your business up and sell it, you can do that too. Your goals should drive the shape of your business. Your goals should include the lifestyle you want, and your business should reflect that. There will always be a correlation on some level as to what you put in and what you get out. It will be very difficult to work five hours a week and earn $1 million a year. What you put in and how you invest your time and efforts will directly correspond to what you get out of your business.

Again, if your business is a constant grind with never ending problems and challenges that seem to always be smothering you, then you are doing it wrong. There is a better way. You can build your business to be in alignment with your goals and vision. It might take time to transition, but it is possible. If you doubt this then ask yourself this question: "Is every landscape business owner having the exact same experiences as me? Do they all struggle the same way I do?" The answer is obviously no, and there are a lot of things you can do about it starting with building your business to match your goals.

Live a Healthy Lifestyle

Have you ever driven through a very affluent neighborhood or part of town and noticed how many people are out jogging, walking, biking or some other healthy physical activity? While there are plenty of successful people who are not healthy, there is a direct correlation between success and a healthy body and mind. Starting with the discipline that it takes to remain healthy.

It's easy to eat whatever you want whenever you want and never exercise, but it takes commitment and discipline to eat right and exercise, and with this discipline comes positive results. The point is not that all healthy people are successful and wealthy, because they are not, but by choosing to live a healthy lifestyle and making conscious decisions to improve your life, you will naturally carry these good habits and disciplines into your business which will contribute to your lasting success.

Develop a Positive Self-Image

Dr. Maxwell Maltz, in his legendary self-improvement book, *Psycho-Cybernetics*, said, "The self-image then controls what you can and cannot accomplish, what is difficult or easy for you, even how others respond to you just as certainly and scientifically as a thermostat controls the temperature in your home." He goes on to say, "You cannot long outperform or escape your self-image. If you do escape briefly, you'll be 'snapped back,' like a rubber band, extended between two fingers, coming loose from one."

This concept is by far the most important lesson in this book, and I know from personal experience. No matter how much of this book you study, no matter how many hours you spend in the office, not matter how much money you invest into marketing, at the end of the day it's your self-image that will determine your ultimate results. Period.

I love learning. I love trying new things. I do not fear much and I have always been willing to take a risk. I have a degree in Landscape Architecture and I provide very professional services. On the surface, I should have made a lot of money early in life. I worked as many hours as anyone and I knew what I was doing. But somehow, someway I always ended up back in the same tax bracket with the same amount of income and the same amount of debt year after year. I could not figure it out and it was frustrating for many years.

I always knew that I did not see myself on level with ultra-successful people. I always felt slightly uncomfortable around very affluent environments and very successful people. My self-image told me that I did not belong and therefore I didn't. I had programmed myself to believe that I had to struggle to succeed, and that it would take a very long time. And just as I believed, I lived.

Over the course of time I became tired of this game, of the struggle of not getting ahead, and eventually I doubled down on myself and invested in developing my self-image. I began to believe that I deserved better. I began having confidence in my talents and believing that I could reach my goals and sure enough, within less than one year, everything began to change for the better. And the best part was, once the tide changed for me, it just grew and grew in the positive direction. Now I know I can accomplish anything. Now I know my ideas, talents and experiences are of value to this world, and it's my duty to share them and make this world a better place, one landscape at a time and one person at a time. I now have a positive, strong and healthy self-image and no matter what circumstances surround me, I know I have the ability to reach my goals and live the life I desire.

I share this very personal and intimate experience with you because I know it can help you too. If you are struggling to have the life you so desire, I invite you to be honest and evaluate your self-image. Do you feel positive and confident about yourself? Do you believe that you deserve and command success? Are your goals in alignment with your self-image? If not, then take efforts to learn more about your self-image and how you can strengthen it.

Don't Go At It Alone

In closing, I want to leave you with this last bit of advice. Being an entrepreneur is often a very lonely position to put yourself in. It's just part of the deal. To step out into the world as an entrepreneur and attempt to make a difference, you are going to feel alone at times. It's your baby and nobody else is going to help you keep it healthy. It's up to you. But that doesn't mean that you must go at it alone. There is always someone who has traveled your path before you or going down the road beside you who can offer support I urge you to reach out to your industry and your local business community and connect with people, find a mentor and build a team around you who can support you.

Make sure you check out the last two pages of this book where you can learn more about The Strategic Landscaper Coaching Program.

Remember, *creating your own landscape economy* is about building a lifestyle. It's about reaching your goals. It's about going places you only dreamed of. The time is now. You have everything you will ever need right between your ears. Challenge yourself: think and use your creative imagination to help you each day. Find the ideas, information and resources you need to grow and live the life you dream of. Look around. It is happening for so many other people every day, and it can happen for you. Believe in yourself, love yourself and make it happen.

To your success!

Bibliography

Kennedy, D. (2013). *NO B.S. Direct Marketing.*
United States of America: Entrepreneur Press.

Are You Ready to Create Your Own Landscape Economy?

A landscape business is an opportunity to create financial freedom, security, peace of mind and most of all a lifestyle that supports your goals and vision.

- Has your business hit a ceiling?
- Are you always struggling to keep up?
- Does payroll stress you out?
- Do you feel like your business owns you instead of you owning your business?
- Do you want to have more time off to spend with your family and on vacation?

If your business is struggling with these issues you are not alone. Unfortunately, many landscape entrepreneurs face these problems year after year. It's only the select few who figure out how to create their own landscape economy and build a lifestyle business that supports their goals and vision.

The Strategic Landscaper Coaching Program Can Help!

Our monthly coaching program is a one to one mentoring and strategic planning system customized to put you on the fast track to achieving your goals and creating the lifestyle business you deserve.

All coaching clients will be personally mentored by Matt Hudson. Coaching includes an annual strategic plan, monthly strategic plan updates, bi-monthly phone calls, unlimited email support, free downloads, resources and much more.

Note: Application Process Required. Not all applications are guaranteed to be accepted. Limited availability.

Learn More at:
StrategicLandscaper.com/coaching

www.ingramcontent.com/pod-product-compliance
Lightning Source LLC
Chambersburg PA
CBHW051703170526
45167CB00002B/517